Life in God's Fast Lane

Spirituality of a Mother

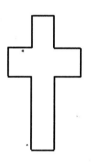

Theresa Brotherton

PublishAmerica
Baltimore

First printing

ISBN: 1-4137-6591-2
PUBLISHED BY PUBLISHAMERICA, LLLP
www.publishamerica.com
Baltimore

Printed in the United States of America

THIS BOOK IS DEDICATED

TO MY GOD AND KING,

GIVER OF ALL GOOD THINGS.

Acknowledgment

I would like to thank Tim, my husband and soul mate, for always being by my side and sharing our crazy lives with the world, just in case this is what God wants. For teaching me many lessons about being a mother, and for the incredible joy they bring to my life, I would like to thank my children, Annie, Timmy, Jacob, and Patrick. I also want to thank my good friend Bishop Gregory, for helping me uncover the courage to dust off my pen and write. Finally, I want to thank all the mothers, everywhere, who share in my journey.

Motherhood

I approached motherhood with the calm confidence that I approached just about everything else in my life. I had two education degrees, read numerous books on parenthood, and knew absolutely what I *wasn't* going to do, from watching everyone else around me. I could figure out trigonometry problems, organize school functions, and I had a good solid head on my shoulders. Simply speaking, I figured that I was already one step ahead of the other mothers already. We brought our beautiful baby girl home from the hospital on a beautiful sunny day in May. My husband was leaving to go to the store soon after we arrived home, when I asked him, "You're not leaving me alone with her, are you?" Panic-stricken, I sat cross-legged on my bed, and marveled at this tiny life that had come from inside of me. I looked down at her fragile face and her tiny hands, and was hit with the sudden realization that I had absolutely no idea of how to be a mother.

Thirteen years and now four children later, I have learned much about motherhood. I have learned that sometimes I don't know anything at all about being a mother, and sometimes I know everything. I have learned that some days my only weapon is prayer. I have learned that children don't come with instructions in neat tidy packages, and I have learned that by the time you figure something out, it is time to move on. I have also learned not to judge other mothers, because often *my* best isn't nearly good enough. I know that babies don't break, and that a box of Fruit Loops, eaten in the van, on the run, can be called breakfast if it is still morning. Good mothers don't have to know how to iron, and, once in awhile, it is okay to have hot fudge sundaes for dinner.

Being a mother has taught me that my heart shares the same worries and carries the same battle scars as millions of other mothers'. And as much as I compare and analyze, a mother's heart is still a mother's heart, no matter what language she speaks. Motherhood means loving until it hurts, and worrying all of the time. It is about not having nearly enough patience, and giving up and starting over a million times in one day. Motherhood is sometimes being a doctor, sometimes a lawyer, always Indian Chief, and a mother's prayers always begin and end for her children.

I've learned that the hardest part of motherhood is letting go. It is the hardest because the letting go part seems almost alien to what our job should be. But I have learned, and am still learning, that God is the Creator, and I am simply the caretaker. His plan for my children looms heavily over all my thoughts, dreams, and wishes for them. And, in the end, after all the endless worrying, planning, and suffering, there really isn't a more beautiful place for them to be in, than in His hands.

So, when I begin to compare myself to other mothers, and weigh and measure what it means to be a good mother, I realize that sometimes a good mother is everything that I'm not, sometimes all that I am, but always everything that I want to be.

Light the Damned Candle

When you become a parent, you are proven wrong in just about everything you believed about parenthood. I had to eat my words when I said, long ago, that my children will never eat cookies for breakfast, play video games, or forget their manners. Sometimes, all I had in the house to eat were cookies, and my words will forever echo in my mind, "Go play a video game."

But as parents, we are forever trying to make things better, teach values, and somehow make God a part of our lives. I look at my children and wonder how I am ever going to help them understand just how much my faith is a part of my life. Words are almost too much for most children. I know that my example and how we live, play a much more important role for them. And knowing that they are watching all that I do is a scary thought that brings me to my knees most days. My plans are always too big. My children always manage to ground me and bring my utopian view of family prayer back to real life. But, as stubbornness is a good trait of most parents, I haven't stopped trying. I figure by the time I am done trying everything, they will be grown and thinking of ways to make their faith a part of their own children's lives. Maybe this continuous circle of trial and error with family prayer is God's plan after all.

When we had a baby in the house, just getting to Sunday Mass was a feat in itself. I used to pretend in my mind that the devil was trying everything in his power to prevent us from making it to church. So the battle was on.

My husband's eyes were often full of doubt when I'd say, "We can make it." We lost shoes. The baby needed to be fed. We forgot the diaper bag. Cheerios spilled all over the van. Blush and eye shadow were kept in the glove compartment along with deodorant and a hairbrush. I learned to tie shoes while I was bent over the back seat, and sometimes flossed my teeth at red lights. We were never early. We were often miserable. I was often exhausted by just getting to church, and not ready for the next battle of keeping everyone happy and content during the service. But I'd always think, in my head, that somehow we'd won!

As they got older, I tried other things. I taught my children how to pray the rosary, when they were old enough to tell me that they couldn't fall asleep alone in their beds. If they still couldn't fall asleep, they could come and get me. Saying it loud enough for us to hear was often a part of their plan to let us know that they weren't asleep yet. I was called because their rosary was broken from constant yanking, or was lost under a tangle of blankets and pillows. Sometimes they couldn't remember just how to say the prayers. Their fingers got confused and they lost their place. They were winning. My plans changed from a whole rosary to one decade, remembering my own mother's words that their guardian angel would finish their rosary for them if they ever fell asleep. This way they could use their ten fingers or ten toes, whichever they chose. My own rosary became a mixed up assortment of Hail Marys and Our Fathers, as I traveled from room to room, because by the time I finally got into my own bed, I was exhausted.

My next plan was a family rosary every night. Complaints were fired at me from every direction. My husband's silence told me it was too much. Plans were scaled down. We would just try a family rosary once a week Sunday night seemed like the best time. We maneuvered around bath time and favorite television shows. We argued about who would be first. Rosaries were fought over. Prayers were said so fast that I could hardly decipher them, or so slowly that I could barely follow. I was determined. I made new rules. No one could sit within touching distance of one another. No one was allowed to talk unless it was his or her turn. (This included grunts, sighs, and moans.) My husband's glance told me I had forgotten why we were doing this. It was my three-year-old's turn. He began, "Hail Mary, full of poop..." Laughter filled the room. My boys became a heap of tangled bodies. My husband turned his rosary in. I gave up.

When my daughter was preparing to receive her first Holy Communion, I came up with a new plan. Since she was the first, I decided we would light a candle at the dinner table each night, so we would remember that she was preparing to receive the most awesome sacrament, and we could remember her in our prayers. Each night before our prayer at the table, my husband would light the candle. I was certain that this simple gesture would be the ideal for our family. I couldn't have been more wrong. My youngest sang "Happy Birthday" each night. Napkins became a fire hazard. Arguments began about who would blow out the candle after dinner was over. I could feel the breeze of my middle son's breath as he talked, trying his best to "accidentally" blow out the candle before dinner was over. My patience lasted about one week. On the eighth night, an argument began about seating arrangements. I could barely hear myself think. I yelled to my husband across the table, "Just light the damned candle!" He gave me the look. I gave up.

Now that my children are older, I am roughly on plan M. I try to make it into their rooms before they go to bed, and just simply pray. Sometimes we just talk, sometimes we say a decade of the rosary together, and sometimes we just listen. They usually interrupt with something that they forgot to tell me about their day, and it is always the time when I find out about someone getting in trouble at school, or a friend being mean. There is no order to how we begin, and no big plans. Sometimes I leave wondering if we really prayed at all. It is crazy and unpredictable, and it seems *mostly* to work, because it fits in perfectly with our lives.

The Mercy Rule

One of the many joys of parenthood is watching your children play sports. I have sat at countless ball games, melted in the summer, and froze on the bleachers at soccer games that have been scheduled when the weather was too cold even to let the dog out. I have listened to parents yell louder than the coaches, watched coaches that forgot to learn the rules of sportsmanship, and have eaten more stale popcorn and cold nacho cheese than I want to admit. I have shared in the joys only winning can bring, and wiped tears from faces when losses came too hard and fast. Sports are good for us. Besides, learning about teamwork and sportsmanship, my children learn that there are just some things in life that you cannot change, no matter how hard you try. One lesson I seem to repeat over and over, is that sometimes you win, and sometimes you lose. Unfortunately, they learn, also, that sometimes you win them all, and sometimes you can lose every time too.

There are also many lessons about life that I can learn as a parent, if I am willing to open my eyes enough to see beyond what is happening on the field.

Last summer, while sitting in the bleachers, I learned an important lesson about God's great love for us. My son's baseball team was in a losing streak. It didn't matter how hard they tried, because they just kept losing. The innings were endless, because the other team just couldn't seem to stop hitting the ball and running home. There was just no hope for our team, and when I was certain I couldn't bear to see the faces of our players get any more frustrated, the umpire ended the game with "the mercy rule."

I breathed a sigh of relief, even though the game was called in the fifth inning. Even though they lost again, our boys were able to salvage a little of the dignity they lost. Their frustration had ended and they could go home angry, hanging their heads, and complaining about who was at fault. I knew that they would kick the dirt, and slam the van doors, and pout the whole way home. And after all of the whining, and blaming, I knew too, that they would forget all their disappointment by the time their next game rolled around, and they would be hopeful, once more, that they could win.

I couldn't help thinking that God has a "mercy rule" for us, too. When we are losing too badly and feel like we can't bear any more, all we have to do is call time out and put His Mercy Rule into play. He always lets us come home. He is waiting and watching for us. He wants us, even with our heads hanging down, when we're whining and complaining about who was at fault. He wants us with our stubbornness and our bad tempers. He smiles at us when we realize that we have nothing to give, and He watches for us to turn our eyes to Him. He is waiting for us to fall down on our knees, kicking the dirt, angry and frustrated. He is waiting to pick us up and shake the dust from our clothes. His loving mercy is there to heal our broken hearts, and to wipe the hot, angry tears from our eyes. He is there when we slam the van door, and when we pout the whole way home. He reads our hearts when words are not enough to tell Him how we're hurting. He waits to open his loving arms and send us His grace, without question. His mercy is enough. His love makes us new. Then, we too, can forget, and be ready for the time the next game rolls around, hopeful and stronger.

St. Francis

There is a small statue of St. Francis of Assisi on my desk. It is chipped and he is missing one of his hands, from constant touching and dropping him. But that is what happens when something is loved and touched by little hands. I am sure he doesn't mind, though, because he is one of the great saints. I think he fits in well with our house, because of his great love for all of God's creatures.

It is easy to love children and animals. We had our first dog long before we had children, and I often think, sometimes, he is one of my biggest fans. Each time I was pregnant, I sat nauseated in the bathroom for most of the morning. My husband would be off to work, and the novelty of watching Mommy throw up got old, so my children soon left me in peace. My only loyal companion was my golden retriever, and if God gave dogs the ability to be compassionate, I am sure he was sharing in my misery, because he is the only one who joined me every day, of every one of my pregnancies, and didn't ask me to open a bag of chips or peel an orange while I was vomiting.

I always envisioned having a house full of children and animals, so I was lax when my children started whining and begging for pets. We have had quite an assortment: dogs, cats, birds, gerbils, hamsters, fish, turtles, ant farm, worm farm... They have made our house much crazier, caused much havoc with everyone, and have taught my children many wonderful lessons that they would have never learned without pets.

They have learned that if you don't pick up dog poop, you will step in it some time, no matter how careful you are. I think this is a good life lesson. My husband rolls his eyes. Much to his dismay, he is an excellent shoe cleaner, and although he would tell you differently, he is as much as an animal lover as I am. He often complains that his main job around our house is "janitor," and since this is the same man who drove two hundred miles with a puppy sitting on his lap, I just have to laugh. When we got engaged, he gave me a bird as a gift. I told him I was sick of the bird spitting seeds all over my bedroom, so he bought me another one, claiming the bird was lonely and now that he had a companion, all would be well. I now had double the singing and double the mess. I think this was an omen for our future family.

The problem comes with everyone in our family not sharing the same "level" of animal lover. When our boys were little, we couldn't resist the charm of the "ant farm." My daughter was afraid of them and didn't understand why we had bugs as pets. The plastic containers of ant farms aren't too sturdy. When the box is dropped, ants and dirt come spilling out all over the floor. We, of course, know this first hand, because our little ant house split into three pieces. We hot-glued the plastic back together with a hot glue gun, but had an extremely difficult time hunting down hundreds of ants to put back in their home. Every time the boys looked away, I tried to stomp on as many as I could, while they yelled, "Careful we don't step on them..." Worm farms are better, because worms run slowly, but their homes are made of Styrofoam.

When my daughter was six years old, she wanted a kitten. We had visions of a little kitten curled up on her pink comforter, soundly sleeping. The first time I brought the kitten home, she screamed in terror. The dog barked at her screaming, and the kitten climbed on top of my head and dug her nails into my scalp. The cat hissed at everyone. My two-year-old son hissed at the cat. The dog growled at the kitten. I was positive everyone could learn to get along. The next day, I discovered our lovely houseguest had brought fleas with her. This entailed one panicked phone call to my husband at work, the children and I moving out for two days, and my husband wearing the "janitor" hat once again. By the time the cat and house were cleaned up, and the dog got used to sharing his space with an enemy, my husband discovered he was allergic to the cat. When we told the children our cat would have to leave, two cheered and two cried. "Fluffy" now lives in sunny Arizona, with one of my former students. We always manage to think of her when the temperature drops below ten degrees.

My husband and I both believe that a pet teaches responsibility. I also believe that tolerating our children learning responsibility can make us crazy. Fish are good pets, we decided. They don't eat too much, make any noise, or make too much of a mess. I *used* to think they were the perfect pets, until we lost one for a week. I discovered he was missing when putting socks away in my son's room. We turned the house upside down looking for the lost fish, and I even began to question my own sanity. People look at you kind of funny when you tell them you lost a fish. A couple days later, my youngest asked me why "Goldie" was so hard. He thought the fish was too cold, so he put him in his drawer, covered him up, and even sprinkled fish food around him. "Goldie" had a great fish burial, and my son learned that fish don't get cold and they need water to live. I learned that fish can get lost, and the next time I am questioning my sanity, I will look in my son's top drawer.

Losing a hamster is a little more understandable. When this happened in our home, my daughter was more upset than anyone. She barricaded herself in her room, and threatened to move in with her aunt. She even called our pet a "rodent." We searched with flashlights, and set traps with food. The hamster jolted us out of bed when he ran across our bedroom rug at 12:00 p.m., and caused me to shriek when he grazed my foot at five o'clock one morning while I was making coffee. My husband, janitor, shoe cleaner, and hamster finder, played Catch-the-Hamster for the next few nights, until "Goldie #2" was safe in his cage. My sons thought he looked sad after tasting freedom for a few days. I thought he was lucky to be alive.

I am certain St. Francis must be smiling when he watches all of God's creatures, whether they are children or animals. When we say bedtime prayers, we always try to remember everything and everyone that needs our prayers. My children hope there is a special place in heaven for all the hamsters, birds, fish, worms, and other animals that have blessed our home. I pray that God especially watches over all of the "beasts and the children." They are the innocent ones. They may all be double the mess, but they are double the singing for me, too.

A Mother's Rosary

Praying the rosary has always been an important part of my life. Naturally, when I became a mother, I thought I would finally share in the same worries and joys that our Blessed Mother must have felt when she became a mother, so I knew that praying the rosary would just become a more perfect prayer for me. I always carried a beautiful crystal rosary everywhere I went.

I was used to praying the rosary alone, or in a quiet room, with my husband sleeping silently next to me. When I was worried or afraid, I inadvertently began saying Hail Marys. They calmed me down. They kept me sane and safe. I knew that my heavenly mother was watching over me and I trusted in her care. I had no idea that my peaceful prayer would be shattered by the little miracles we created

My first foray into motherhood began when I was in labor for the first time. I brought my rosary along, thinking I would pray Hail Marys instead of doing the breathing exercises I had learned. Plan A went right into the trash, along with everything that I had learned in Lamaze Class. I was sweating, nauseated, and in pain. My beautiful rosary looked like the perfect weapon, because every time my husband spoke, I wanted to throw it right at his head. I cursed, I swore, I threw up, and not one Hail Mary managed to leave my lips. I knew that I had much to learn.

A newborn baby turned my world upside down. She cried and I said Hail Marys. She nursed and I said Hail Marys. My nightly rosary became a garbled murmur of

Hail Marys and Our Fathers, sleepily said aloud. I'd wake up to find my rosary tangled around a pacifier or lost in blankets. It couldn't survive the wear and tear and finally broke. I bought a cheap plastic one. This fit more into the role of motherhood than crystal anyway.

While in labor with my second child, I managed to squeeze out a few Hail Marys between curses. My plastic rosary was held tight in my fist. It felt good there. When our son was born, I often had two sleeping children on my lap. There wasn't a more perfect place for them to be, but I no longer had a hand in which to hold a rosary. I looked down at our son, and laughed. God had a reason for making ten fingers and ten toes on newborns. I prayed my rosary, but I lost count every time he had to burp. I said too many Hail Marys for each decade, and lost my place more then I knew where I was, because there didn't seem to be an order any more. But this seemed to match my life, so I wasn't worried.

Finally, ready for my third child, I said Hail Marys driving to the hospital, and throughout his birth. When he was born, the doctor laid his head on my chest, and I moved my rosary out of the way so it wouldn't hurt his fragile head. I was a mother for the third time and the Blessed Mother hadn't let me down. With a four-year-old, a two-year-old, and a newborn, life became more beautiful and crazy all at once. My plastic rosary, now one of many, became a necklace for my daughter. My children played with them, smashed them into Playdoh, and took them apart. We took them to church. The Easter Bunny and Santa Claus always remembered to bring a rosary. Hail Marys were my mother's mantra. The words were so ingrained in my brain; I didn't even have to move my lips at all. I rarely had time to sit down and actually hold one, but I hung one in almost every room of my house, and often glanced at them as I said Hail Marys while I did my chores.

When I was pregnant with my fourth child, I had a difficult pregnancy. Six weeks before I was due, I was sent to the hospital from a routine doctor's appointment.

Admitted to the labor floor, with only my car keys and wallet, I prayed my Hail Marys silently. I was crying and worried. My rosary was at home. I borrowed my dad's. It was metal, and the heavy beads felt good, because I knew that his hands had prayed this rosary many times. The Hail Marys became steady with my heartbeat. My doctor was worried that one of us wouldn't make it. I thought of my three children at home, and the one growing inside of me. Helpless, I turned to the blessed mother and gave her my unborn son. "Take him for your own and protect him in case I am not here," I prayed. "He is yours." I knew she would understand. She is a mother.

Too many drugs blurred my prayers. I couldn't remember if I had a rosary, or just couldn't find it. I drifted in and out of sleep. Later, miraculously, our baby boy was born.

He was tiny and beautiful and perfect. The next few hours, I was pretty out of it. When I woke up, my nurse was hanging my dad's rosary from my IV pole. She said it must have dropped out of my hand because she found it on the floor.

Our fourth child was a perfect addition to our crazy house. I have counted Hail Marys on his fingers while I fed him, and said them half asleep in the middle of the night, praying he would go to sleep. They have been my hope and consolation through surgery, sickness, and worry. I have found rosaries in the washing machine and between couch cushions. They are cracked and broken and full of crumbs. One was stuck in a wad of bubble gum, and another sucked up in the vacuum cleaner. I pick them up, kiss the cross, and hang them from doorknobs, or stick them in my pocket. I cannot bear to throw them away. They are too much a part of me.

Adoration, for a Mother

Adoration, for a mother, is finding God all day, in everything
And adoring Him in anyone you touch.

It is praising Him when you hear the sound of children waking up and bare feet running down the hall.

It is getting up early to make the house smell like pancakes, and later, silently and impatiently scraping cold, sticky syrup off of the chairs.

It is a gentle hand guiding newborn lips to swollen breasts, and caressing tiny feet to coax him to eat.

It is in adoring tiny fingers and toes, while making the kitchen sink into a bubble bath for chubby legs, and rubbing creamy pink lotion on velvet skin.

Adoration, for a mother, smells like peanut butter and jelly,
And suntan lotion on a summer day.

It is the popping of fresh popcorn, and the sound of excited giggles while you turn the living room into a movie theatre for movie night.

It is turning off the stove to have a tiny tea party on the kitchen floor, with red Kool-Aid and graham crackers.

It is hearing God's voice as you close your eyes and listen with your heart, as she reads her first book.

It is a silent prayer as you run into his room to check if he is still breathing, when he just slept through the night for the first time.

It is His heart you share when she has a bad dream and her cry jolts you awake.

Adoration is running after his bike, yelling, "Don't stop pedaling!" as you let go for the first time.

It is the panic of the first visit to the emergency room, and it is giving him your strength, by squeezing his hand and staring into his eyes because your words will never be enough.

It is the quiet pleading to God, "Let me suffer, not her."

Adoration, for a mother, means eating runny eggs and burned toast on Mother's Day, and asking for seconds.

It means searching for Him as she screams, "I hate you," and begging for the patience to say the right words as she slams the door to her room.

Adoring Him, in them, means sopping up water because it was his turn to do the dishes. It is hearing the clanking of Legos that were sucked up in the vacuum hose, and finding Him in the colicky crying of your baby, as you rock him with the constant hum of the dryer, to calm him down.

It is the joy in your heart as your son's belly laugh rings through the house, and it is clenching your teeth and keeping your closed fists behind your back to hide your anger, because you are their teacher.

It is the silent prayer of thanks that you were there to see him hit his first home run, and unending gratitude that they are able to laugh and run and be free.

Adoration, for a mother, means constantly searching for God in them, and giving your life to them because you love them. It is praising Him because they are God's eyes and heart and song, in a tangible, lovable, kissable creation. It is struggling to find God in them because you are impatient and frustrated and tired. Adoration is stroking his hair and asking for her forgiveness. It means starting over again and vowing to be a better mother.

It is unending and tiring and noisy and beautiful.

Grass

I am not able to grow both children and grass at the same time. I have tried, but unfortunately, grass doesn't grow by good intentions. Neither do children. Which is why I try to focus on being a mother instead of a lawn specialist. Our front lawn is missing big patches of grass in strategic places. If you bend your head sideways, you can see that there isn't any grass growing where home plate, first, second, and third base should be. My three sons don't seem to notice the condition of our lawn. They only see a miniature baseball field, and love to tap their bats and grind their cleats into the dirt, to make dust fly up in the air. My youngest is obsessed with sliding as he runs to every base. I know he envisions himself as a professional baseball player, because he told me that his batting stance is the same as one of the Cardinals' players'. Every year, we have planted grass, and nursed and watered those tiny seeds. And every year, I fall behind in my duty of grass protector, and one of our children forgets and manages to step on those fragile blades of grass. They would yell, "Dad is going to get mad," and I would try to pry those little green blades up out of the dirt, mumbling to myself, "I am raising children, not grass." It didn't take very much for me to lose my patience and give up.

I used to dread the spring because I knew that my husband would say it was time to plant grass seed. Last year, I tried to get the inevitable over with, and bought him a bag of grass seed for Father's Day. After I convinced him that I wasn't being mean, he worried me by saying that he has given up trying to grow grass when our children (plus an assortment of neighborhood children) use our lawn as a gathering place for their games.

It took me a few minutes to decide if he was really serious or not. I know our front lawn bothers him, because he thinks it is an eyesore to our neighbors. But he knows that the sound of children gathered around our house is music to my ears, and I think my husband has learned to close his eyes when he walks to the front door every day. He is convinced that people with plush green lawns must have bad marriages, and I am convinced of how much he has given up just for me, because he walks through the dust at home plate to get to our front door every day, and doesn't say a word. And that bag of grass seed lays unopened on the shelf in our garage, gathering dust.

I know it will be a different story once our children are older. My daughter already complains about the condition of our lawn. I suggested she get dropped off at the neighbor's house and walk around to the back of our house. That way none of her friends will know exactly which house is ours, or which lawn. This sounds much easier to me than actually trying to grow grass again.

When we first moved into this house, I couldn't wait for my children to climb down to the creek, and enjoy the woodsy area around our house. Of course, the first thing they did was to throw rocks to hear the splash of water. Our older next-door neighbor had a hard time seeing the creek rocks disturbed, and complained to me. He was afraid the rocks would fall on his lawn. I told him the main reason we moved here was for our boys to be able to throw rocks in the creek, but we would be careful not to disturb his grass. And I told him when our children were grown, Tim and I would just sit and enjoy the grass and rocks, but now, we were raising children, so it is hard to sit and enjoy anything.

We wrote him an apology note, thinking it is bad policy to make enemies of your neighbors the first week. We tried to be careful, but he still turns his head when we wave. I wonder if he remembers being ten years old.

I am hoping that when our children are grown, grass will eventually fill in the dust of those bases on our lawn. The thought of a quiet and beautiful lawn, with no bats, cleats, or soccer cones spread around, seems peaceful, and sad. I wouldn't mind a beautiful lawn, and my husband has certainly earned a great one, but I can't imagine spending my day taking care of grass, or sitting still long enough to enjoy it. But then again, no one really knows if I am capable of growing grass, so my worries may all be in vain.

"It's a Mother Thing"

"It's a mother thing." I used these words the first time when our daughter was six weeks old and going to the store with her father for the first time. He was a great father, and so excited to show the world his new daughter, but I felt like I had a lead weight on my chest. She hadn't been out of my sight for a minute yet, and I wasn't ready to let go.

I clenched my teeth, looked right at the man I loved and trusted more than anyone in the world, and quickly said to him, "Don't forget to take her out of the car."

I closed my eyes so I wouldn't have to see the expression on his face, but I heard him answer through clenched teeth, "Do you think I am an idiot?"

I trusted him completely, but my heart was full of worries that I didn't have words for.

"I'm sorry," I quickly added. " I just had to say it—it's just a mother thing."

He shook his head and I felt like an idiot, but he accepted my excuse without question. They left. I worried the whole time they were gone.

So my words, "it's just a mother thing" are now an integral part of my vocabulary. They spill out of my mouth when what I am doing doesn't seem to make sense, when I don't have a good reason or the time to explain anything. The more the mommy stuff creeps into my life and changes me into the woman that I am today, the more it just makes sense to me, and the more I accept that it *always* doesn't make sense to anyone else.

29

These words have worked when I really don't have the right answer or explanation for how I am feeling, and they have given me courage to step in and do what needs to be done, regardless of stares and judgments from others.

"It's a mother thing" means that I write my cell phone number on my son's arm with a permanent marker before camp, because I am worried he may get sick and not be able to tell someone my phone number.

It means I mumble Hail Marys as I sit in the bleachers, because it is his first time, ever, at bat, and he has been waiting all year to run to first base.

It means that I lose my temper when I am expected to accept mediocrity where my children are concerned, and that I can be ruthless when role models for my children don't live up to my expectations.

It means after I watch the news, I hug and kiss them for no reason.

"It's a mother thing" means when crazy people are crashing planes into buildings, I drive to school, sit in the parking lot, and pray the rosary to make sure my children are safe.

"It's a mother thing" means I pray for rain because I need to be at two places at one time.

It means I drop them off, say "I love you," and when I am finally alone, I miss them and can't stop thinking about them.

A "mother thing" means if I have a bad dream, I find them, to listen to them breathe; and if they have a bad dream, they climb into our bed and sleep next to me, and I whisper "You are safe," until they are asleep again.

"It's a mother thing" means sometimes I drive my husband crazy because I have a feeling that something is not right. It means if I blink, tears will fall from my eyes for no reason. It means we will be ready to go and I won't leave, or sometimes I will wake him up and tell him, "I just wish they were all home." But when he says he will go pick them up, I tell him no.

It means when I give him a *look*, he will drive, check, bring, or deliver something, without question, for them, just because my heart is restless.

"It's a mother thing" means the smell of a newborn baby brings tears to my eyes.

It means nothing will take away my pain when I do not have what my children need.

"It's a mother thing" means I understand completely that there are only two kinds of people in the world: mommies and *not* mommies, and babies can tell the difference.

"It's a mother thing means" I am stone and steel, but am crushed by the realization that no one loves them as I do. So I can never let go, or give up, or give in.

"It's a mother thing" is a feeling, a way of thinking, a simple explanation for a complicated commitment to give up a part of myself for them.

Fifteen years later, I sometimes still look in the eyes of the man I love and trust, and tell him, "It's a mother thing." He still silently shakes his head and accepts my explanation. I don't know if he really understands, or he is just still too leery to mess with a "mother thing."

Caitlin's Mom

We both signed up to volunteer at our school. All the parents of children participating in the sports program had to do a day of duty. It was usually the mothers who volunteered. I was wondering whom I would be working with, and I hoped she would be someone who knew what she was doing. I didn't know her name, but I could see her coming from a mile away. The bleached tips of her spiked hair stood straight up as she sauntered into the concession stand. She had her ear pierced up the side, and the stubs of her fingernails were painted a bright red. Although it was cold, she wore tight, faded jeans and sandals, with a white t-shirt tucked in. Her toenails matched the blood red of her fingernails, and my first thought when I looked at her was, *How could* she *be somebody's mother?* She didn't look like a mother. She looked tough. Like she had been around the block and could take care of herself very well. But I couldn't see how she fit in with making dinner and studying multiplication tables and reading bedtime stories. Where were her khaki pants, school sweatshirt and Nike tennis shoes? Didn't she know that mothers should *look* like mothers? I knew lots of mothers, all different, but none like this. I couldn't help thinking that she couldn't be a very good mother if she didn't even *look* like one. I decided that she belonged in a bar, not the concession stand at our school, and after watching her shake my hand and hearing her deep raspy voice, I was certain that she had no business being a mother.

But as we began working together, I found myself being drawn to her dynamic personality. She moved about with an ease and confidence about who she was, and what she was doing. Her great sense of humor was evident every time she made one of the children laugh, and she seemed to have a steady line of young customers waiting to buy nachos and pretzels. The kids thought she was "cool." She told jokes and danced around the concession stand, not caring who was watching her. The sincerity of her smile left everyone she touched, a little brighter and happier. She was so accepting of everything and everyone, easily shaking off what didn't matter, and laughing about what did. I felt badly about my first impression of her as I found myself telling her much about my life, and my own children. She shared my own worries and joys of motherhood; and she really listened to what I had to say, and made my efforts at motherhood seem pretty good.

She had three children of her own. All girls. She regaled stories of birthday party sleepovers and Girl Scout meetings, and homework. She talked about dressing up for the mother/daughter fashion show and trick-or-treating right along with her girls. She didn't seem to care what other people thought of her, but the deep love for her children was evident every time she talked about them. Her oldest wanted to make her own ponytail in the mornings, and just had a sleepover with eight girls. They stayed up all night and made s'mores while they watched movies. Her middle daughter was having trouble with multiplication tables, and she could remember having trouble with the eights and nines when she was in third grade too. They studied flash cards every night, but she didn't think it really mattered too much if her daughter could do all the tables in three minutes like they wanted her to do at school. She rolled her eyes and decided that teachers, sometimes, forgot about everyday living.

Then she turned around and there were a few moments of silence, and her voice became quieter. Her blue eyes betrayed a hint of pain as she started talking about Caitlin. Caitlin was her youngest, and she was born with some physical handicaps and was diagnosed with Autism. Her daughter couldn't attend the Catholic school with her two oldest, but she was enrolled at the area public school, to receive the services they offered to handicapped children. Caitlin could give anyone a hard time, and needed much extra help, so after she was born, Caitlin's mom decided to quit work and make sure that her daughter had just what she needed. After she made breakfast in the morning, she drove her oldest two to school, then had to battle with Caitlin. "Sometimes getting dressed is a battle, and sometimes it is just hard to get her on the bus." She shrugged and laughed like this was a normal routine for everyone. She often found herself at her youngest daughter's school, because the teacher was having a hard time getting her to complete her work. "I am not a teacher," she said, "but I know how smart she is. I want my daughter to have all of the opportunities that everyone else has. If I have to be there day after day, then that is the place where I will be."

She talked about Caitlin's gifts and how she wished that someone else could see and appreciate her beauty. She proudly listed all the things that her daughter finally learned how to do, and how long it took her to learn them.

"I work with her all of the time," she said. "And she is able to do many of the things that everyone thought she couldn't." She also admitted her worries for Caitlin, as she got older, and talked about how much money all of the doctors and specialists cost. "We miss the money from my job sometimes," she said quietly, "but Caitlin is my daughter."

I looked sheepishly at the floor, and was instantly sorry for judging her. I knew that God had picked the perfect mother for Caitlin. Caitlin's mom needed to be tough. She needed to be determined and stubborn. She needed spiked hair and rings on every finger, because she needed not to worry what everyone else thought. Caitlin needed a mom who didn't mind brokenness, because she marched to different music than everyone else, too. She needed a mother who would fight to get her on the bus every morning, and who would paint her fingernails bright red when she came home. Caitlin needed someone to let her brush her own hair, someone to accept and be proud of her efforts. She needed a mother who would dress up like a Spice Girl for Halloween, and act like a kid, so Caitlin could learn to act like a kid, too. She needed a mom who thought teachers didn't understand about everyday life, and didn't mind going to school to show them. Caitlin's mom had to be someone who needed to let the "not important stuff" roll off her shoulders. Caitlin needed a mom who could dance in the concession stand, and laugh out loud, and give up everything else, just to be Caitlin's mom.

I learned a lesson from that spiked-haired woman who didn't look like a mother. I learned that sometimes the best mothers come in wild packages. They are the ones who teach us to embrace life, and don't mind changing the rules as the game is played. Caitlin is a lucky girl.

Band-Aids and Glue

I decided what mothers need the most are glue, band-aids, and the grace to know when something is too broken to be fixed. As mothers, we are constantly fixing things. I've hot-glued a foam ant farm, ceramic elephants, trucks, trains, and the top to the Christmas tree, all back together, and glued Girl Scout badges to the vest. I've hot-glued the hem of a pair of pants before Christmas Eve Mass, and I've super-glued the only glass Christmas ornament we own. I've glued the elbow of one of the three wisemen back onto his shoulder, and adhered wooden hands from a blessed mother statue onto my own thumb. Mothers fix broken toys, dinners, and torn pages of books. We have pieced birthday cakes back together with icing, and have learned to re-string the basketball nets in the driveway. We have strung rosary beads back to the rosary, re-linked necklaces, and patched bicycle tires and soccer balls. We kiss cuts, scrapes and bumps, Band-aid them up when they are bleeding, and drive to the emergency room while holding a wet cloth over a bleeding hole in the back of our child's head.

Mothers find themselves saying, tons of times a day, "We will fix it," or "It's not lost, just misplaced." We've learned how to iron homework when it was too crumpled to turn in, and learned to write letters like a second grader, when frustration was making tears come too fast to stop during homework time. We look at a gallon size can of chili at the supermarket, and think that might be just the right size to hold up the broken rail of a bed until we can fix it, or that might be just the thing to fix for Super Bowl Sunday dinner.

We have fixed the look of doubt on a teacher's face by a simple stare, and fixed frustration and disappointment, by our belief that practice will make it better.

We say, "No problem," when we have no idea what we are going to do, and, "It's going to be okay," when we are crying inside. We've dried wet pants under the dryers in many bathrooms, and dried cell phones and Gameboys when they have fallen into toilets or have accidentally been through the wash cycle of the washing machine. We can take apart computer printers and fix elbows that have come out of the joints, from hanging on swing sets. We know how to fix bubblegum stuck in hair, hurt feelings from friends, and broken hockey sticks, even when they are broken in anger.

So when there is nothing else we can do, when it can't be fixed—that is when we need God's grace to admit that it is out of our control. We need God's grace because we usually don't know how to admit something is out of our control, or how to ask for help, because our job is to keep everything running smoothly and to fix what is broken. When guilt floods through us, and when we are finally quiet and shattered enough to step back and face the brokenness before us—that is when we will grow stronger. And in this strength, comes the grace to face picking up all of the broken parts, one piece at a time. Only then are we finally able to see the beauty that spilled out too.

Humility

If you can learn humility by being humiliated, mothers have cornered the market. As much as I try to do the right things and be the "perfect" mother, my best efforts often melt into the ground, so I have decided that perfection in motherhood is utterly impossible. I've great desires to be the perfect mother, but somehow my children manage to bluntly open my eyes, to let me know that I have failed. The message "MOM IS A DICTATOR" flashes across my computer screen. I leave it there to remind me that my children seldom see things as I do. Much of what I have prayed about and thought out so carefully, is instantly dismissed as "lame." They make me think and rethink what I do. Often, I wonder if God hasn't sent them to be my teacher, instead of the other way around. If they are, then they are doing a pretty good job, because I am still learning. However, one thing about motherhood seems to stay the same. That is, that my imperfection grows, as the day is long, and the older my children are, and the more enmeshed in the world they become, the happier they are to remind me of how often I fall short of "perfection."

Their school shirts don't have the telltale crease that an iron gives. The sandwiches I make for school lunches are not the right kind. And there is often more dust than paint on the family van. My son rolls up the windows in the van, so no one will hear my music. My children worry more about how my clothes look than I do.

I stop and wonder how we got turned around. Just when my children seemed old enough not to embarrass me too much in public, I became an embarrassment to them. This humility thing must be a lifelong learning experience. Yes, I am an embarrassment to them, but sometimes I just simply remind them of how much I have been humiliated by things my children have done. When they were younger, I used to think of them as little time bombs, never quite knowing when they would make me cringe by what they did. So my first lesson of motherhood was to stop trying to hide our crazy lives, because I have discovered that the truth is often more unbelievable than a lie.

My youngest threw up all over our dentist's office. I tried to inconspicuously clean the mess, but the throw-up was rolling down pictures of the dentist's wife and children, not to mention his rubber plant. Also, it's pretty hard to be nonchalant, while vomit is rolling down the inside of your shirt and into your shorts.

As I sat there mortified, and wondering how to recover from this mess, my daughter stuck her head in the room and said, "I heard someone threw up. Of course, I knew it had to be us." I wanted to change our names so they wouldn't remember us, but they had all of our records. The second lesson of motherhood: Live with it.

A friend of mine wonders why I have the number to poison control on speed dial. I tell her because I must spend so much time getting the nurse to believe me, I can't waste dialing time.

"My son ate a stick of deodorant," I mumble into the phone.

"Are you sure?" the nurse asks. "Deodorant tastes too badly for him to have eaten too much."

"No, he actually ate quite a bit," I answer.

"Have you ever tasted deodorant? It's pretty awful."

"Well, I am looking down his throat right now," I say. "And it is coated with white and smells like Secret antiperspirant. He must have done it, because even the dog is too smart to have eaten it, and I can't seem to find it anywhere else in the house."

"Oh, it is Secret antiperspirant," she says. "That won't hurt him."

I have to be nice to the Poison Control Lady. She knows too much about my failures as a mother. She knows that my children have tasted Windex window cleaner, because it looks like blue Kool-Aid and Comet Bathroom cleaner, because the can resembles the Parmesan cheese can we use on spaghetti.

The emergency room nurse is someone else I should bribe for her silence.

"My son stuck a blue m&m up his nose," I told her.

"How do you know?" she asked me.

"Well, because there is blue snot coming out of his nose, and it smells like chocolate."

While I sat there thinking that I wanted to kill him, and worried that the blue m&m would be stuck there forever, he managed to blow the m&m out of his nose.

Another day, we had some Playdoh stuck in an ear.

"How do you know he put Playdoh there?" the nurse asked on the phone.

"Because he told me," I said. " It was Playdoh Day at preschool, and he wanted to bring some home. He didn't have a pocket to bring it home in, so he used his ear."

Her silence made me realize that I was the only one who thought this made perfect sense. It gets worse, because when my son was three, we loved to go to the library and read books, until our neighborhood librarian asked him, "Hello, how are you doing?"

He answered, "Boys have penises, and girls have vaginas."

Two weeks later, at the same library, he accidentally zipped a little of his skin while zipping up his pants in the bathroom. His screams brought everyone running, until I explained that we just had a little zipping accident, and that everyone was okay. People looked at me like zipping accidents weren't everyday occurrences. My library books were quite overdue by the time we went back.

Lesson number three: It never gets any better.

Somewhere along the way, God must have decided that church was a good place for mothers to learn to live with humiliation. Besides dragging them into church whining and complaining, and lugging an endless supply of books and distractions and trying to keep them quiet, you learn that they choose the quietest times to make their move. While on vacation in Kentucky, we attended the Catholic church in Paducah. The pastor had all visitors stand to be welcomed. After the applause died down and we were ready to take our seats, my youngest chose this time to yell "Damn it," because he dropped all of his Cheerios on the floor. My oldest three started laughing and my husband was ready to disown us all. Lesson number four: Just keep silent and smile.

Lent

Another season of Lent rolls around. As usual, I have big plans. I imagine our family quietly praying the rosary together, or reciting the Stations of the Cross. My hope, every year, is that my children are able to understand a little more about the great love Jesus had for us when He died on the Cross. I pray and think about what we will do. I am ready to polish our rosaries, reasoning, that now that my children are older, we will be able to do some bigger things to prepare for the Easter season. I never learn. One look at their faces dries up my enthusiasm immediately. But, God is good to me. I can always manage to begin Lent peacefully. I suggest to my children that they should try and sacrifice something, and also do something for someone else. They want specifics. They want to know just how many good things they need to do. "Just try and do something for God today," I simply explain. My oldest son tells me that he did something for God last Tuesday. I was afraid to ask him if he thought he was finished. I realize that I am not adequately prepared to battle for my faith with my own children. I wonder how I will teach them that our journey to God takes a whole lifetime of prayer and sacrifice, if we can't even get a handle on Lent.

My youngest is ready with a long list of what he will "give up." I try to tell him to pick one thing, but he is determined. After he thinks it over for a while, he comes back and tells me, "Lent doesn't sound fun." He announces that Lent should be for grownups and Christmas for kids, but decides that he will give up his favorite computer game and favorite candy. I decide that Lent is easy when you are five. I look at my older son who, when *he* was five, gave up licking his fingers and sticking them in the sugar bowl. He looks away, not really wanting to commit to too much. I know my son. One year he wanted to give up eating bananas. I couldn't let him do that, since that was one of the few healthy foods he actually ate. He likes to change his sacrifice every few days, so it will fit in more with the free lifestyle that he works so hard to maintain. He snaps his fingers and says, "I'll get back to you." I assure him that I will be asking again. My daughter knows the routine, but decides that her Lenten sacrifice is between her and God. I respect her opinion and am happy God is in charge of someone in this house. She also pleads with me not to give up coffee, because I am too crabby in the morning without at least one cup. Her point is well taken. I silently think, *Let the Lenten games begin.*

By the third week of Lent, things start falling apart. The family Lenten books I bought, are stuck to the kitchen table because someone spilled Kool-Aid on them. I try to pry the pages apart, but they are forever stuck together. I reason that no one is reading them anyway, but I can't bring myself to throw them away. There is a telephone message written on top of Jesus' face on the fifth station of the cross, and the Lenten candle I put on the table has a wad of chewed up bubble gum stuck to it. I have started drinking coffee again, and am just trying to drink it black. My children are counting how many days of Lent there are left. They are sick of eating fish, sick of being nice, and sick of Friday Night Devotion.

"Friday Night Devotion," my older son decided, is what priests thought up to make us miserable. "Don't they have anything better to do?" His complaints last two times longer than the actual service. I wonder if actually making them go to church with me isn't a sacrifice for me, instead of for them. They start on Thursday thinking of excuses not to attend. My oldest two actually manage to miss one. My middle son's clothes itch, because he isn't allowed to wear shorts to church, and he prays for a priest that will talk the fastest. He also times the service, and taps his foot on the pew if it goes beyond twenty-five minutes. He is worried that Devotions are seriously affecting his life. I am worried that they aren't.

By the fifth week of Lent, I have just about given up. I, myself, begin counting the days until Easter, and start worrying about what everyone will wear to church. I can't remember who gave up what, and can't really tell if anyone is doing anything nice for anyone else, either. I finally throw the Lenten books into the trash can, but salvage the Stations of the Cross. I give everyone a reprieve from Friday Night Devotion, and order cheese pizza for dinner. I have given up lighting the Lenten candle, because the wick has melted inside the wax. I give God a glance of remorse as I sit down and have a big cup of coffee with flavored cream.

Patience

Patience eludes me most days. I sometimes wonder if God forgot to give me the full dose, knowing good and well, I would need an amazing amount to be a mother. I accept my limitations. I told my children that I started out with a deficit in the patience area, and often remind them that they have to make do with what I have. I grit my teeth, I smile when I want to scream, and I forge ahead, in my usual fashion, always praying for more, but knowing that life doesn't stop for anyone, whether he has patience or not.

A good friend reminds me that patience is learned, and that God sends His grace only after I have worked hard enough on my own.

"Okay," I told God. "You know what I have; I'm ready to work on the patience thing." I think He must have laughed, knowing that it wouldn't take much to teach me how much I lacked. I ran over a scooter backing out of the driveway. I calmly got out of the van and sent the scooter flying through the garage. Of course, nobody was responsible for leaving it in the driveway. I yelled about responsibility and taking care of your things. I kicked a trash can. It tipped over and sent trash falling all over.

My children were all avoiding me by then, so I sat down on the front step, and mumbled, "Okay, I failed my first test."

The next day, I was determined to do better. I managed to remain calm through one fight at the breakfast table, a lost pair of shoes, and clothes that were still wet in the dryer. I didn't trust myself to say a word. I was wondering whether the "Grace" from God would come down like a thunderbolt, or I would just amazingly turn in to June Cleaver, pearls and all. We found the shoes in the garage, and I blow-dried a sweatshirt in the bathroom, with the hair dryer. I was pretty proud of myself. I looked at the clock. We had only been up for forty-five minutes.

My husband smiled at me, and I snapped, "Don't make this harder than it is."

I felt like I was in an Olympic game, and hundreds of judges with clipboards were just waiting to take marks off of my score. I was handed the telephone in the shower.

My son yelled, "The dog threw up on the rug! It looks like he ate a chocolate candy bar." Someone had left the van door open all night, and I wasn't sure it would still start, but I couldn't find my car keys. My nine-year-old reminded me we had forgotten to study for his spelling test.

"We will study in the van," I yelled. It was only 7:40 a.m.

After dropping off my car pool, and kids, I returned home, grabbed the dry cleaning, my cell phone, and overdue library books. I could make 9:00 a.m. Mass, drop off clothes and books, and make playground duty by 11:40 a.m. I told my five-year-old to get in the van and buckle-up. My cell phone rang. I tripped over a baseball cleat, dropped all the clothes and books, and twisted my ankle. My car keys went flying across the garage.

I called my husband from my cell phone and told him, "I quit."

A whole day of patience was too much. I needed to break this patience thing up into smaller steps. I would live hour-by-hour. I could endure torture for an hour. Labor lasted for more than an hour, and I managed to survive that. I knew this would work. All my children were home for Easter Break, so this would be the true test. My head was face down on the table during breakfast.

My daughter looked sideways at me and I said, "I am trying not to yell for one hour."

"Why save it up, Mom, if you are just going to yell later? Isn't it just better to get it over with?"

My thirteen-year-old made too much sense. We survived breakfast together without too much turmoil, and chores were finished semi-decently. I had made it one whole hour without yelling. Then, we colored eggs for Easter. We fought over who would get what color, and who would sit where. The dog stepped in spilled dye and got blue footprints all over the house. A raw egg was dropped on the pile of unpaid bills and eggshells were all over the kitchen floor. Someone had divided up the cooked eggs unfairly, and a wrestling match began. I didn't yell. I didn't scream. I calmly walked into my bedroom and I punched a hole in my bedroom wall.

"Okay," I said to God, through my tears. "You win. I give up. I don't even have enough patience to begin to try. I can't even begin without You."

There were no miraculous showers of grace that poured into me on that day, and no thunderbolts, but I learned a quiet and valuable lesson. I learned that God is the perfect parent. I mess up and start over as many times as my own children. I fight, and I am selfish and ungrateful. Everything that I do is done imperfectly, and I will never measure up to His perfect plan for my life. But He looks at me through the eyes of a loving father, not an impatient one, and His mercy is so great that I am allowed to begin over again and again, if that is what I need.

So I am still learning patience. Some days, I still don't have enough. But I try to look at my children a little differently now. Before I start yelling and complaining, I try to see them through my Father's eyes, and sometimes when I look at them through these eyes of love, His grace pours into my heart like a thunderbolt, and I have more patience that I can hardly believe.

Say You're Sorry

"Say you're sorry," are words that come out of my mouth thousands of times as a mother. My children try to be tough. They look at me with anger in their eyes and defiance on their face and I know that they aren't one bit sorry. They mumble the words so they won't really count for too much, or say they are sorry with their teeth gritted, and fists clenched, ready for a fight.

I say, "That's a stinky apology," and realize I am at a loss. I am at a loss because teaching them to say they are sorry, and having them *feel* it in their heart, are often two things that are worlds apart. I am at a loss because they often don't know what they did wrong, or won't admit it if they do. And I am at a loss because I think of all of the times that I've met anger with anger, and hurt with hurt, and said that I'm sorry but didn't really mean it, either. So I wonder if a stinky apology beats no apology after all, or if they are the same.

I want to teach my children that life is about messing up, picking up the pieces, and starting all over. But during the inevitable "messing up" part, sometimes we hurt others that have gotten in the way. So, along with this messing up, comes owning up to what we did and saying "sorry."

I remember when my grandmother heard that someone was sad or hurting, she would gently say, "I'm sorry." I used to look at the sincerity in her eyes and wonder why she was apologizing if she didn't do anything wrong. Now, I realize that she was sorry just because someone was upset. She didn't understand much English, but I know that she felt others' pain just from being with them, and could read the hurt in their eyes when she looked at them. It didn't matter what color or shape or size they were, because their beauty was found in simply being children of God. "I'm sorry," for her, meant she was willing to share a little in someone else's journey, no matter what it cost. When she said, "I'm sorry," people would usually melt a little, and pour out many more words to her, than she was capable of understanding.

So I guess my prayer is that my children learn to have the compassion of my grandmother. I want them to know that the kind of "tough" needed in the world today, is to realize when someone is hurting, and to be sorry, whether they are responsible or not. It doesn't take much courage to walk around with clenched fists, ready for a fight, but only the very brave are able to open their eyes and choose to look for the truth. Then, their apologies will come from their heart, and be seen in their eyes; and then it won't really matter who was at fault.

I realize, in frustration, that this lesson is something that is learned through a lifetime, and not in one moment. And I've come to the startling realization that, as my grandmother was for me, I am my children's greatest teacher.

Their compassion will be learned when I am able to open my own fists into outstretched hands, and let my anger fall away. Compassion will be learned when I am able to swallow my own indignation and pride, and choose to hear another side of the story. It will come for my children when they see that I don't care about being "right" more than I care about people. When I can look at another person and just simply see a child of God, created so beautifully in His image, then my compassion will pour from my heart and shine in my eyes. Then they will learn.

Maybe they will just stop and think a little about what my actions mean, and why I am choosing this way. Maybe they will just question the way things are. It may take many such moments for them to understand, or maybe it will take a whole lifetime. But, it is too important a lesson to wait. It is something that our weary world cries out for every day. And like my grandmother, who didn't know many big words or have great explanations for things, "I'm sorry," will be enough.

Letting Go

Eat right. Exercise. Pray for a healthy baby. Read the book to be a good mother. Get the room ready. Can you feel him move? Protect him. Fold the diapers. Try not to worry. Pick a name. Give it all up for her. Feel him kicking. Wait and see. Be patient. Breathe.

Let go and push her out.

Watch his head. Let me feed her. She likes to burp lying across my lap. Do you think she is eating enough? Is he hungry? We'll be late because the baby has to nurse. Should I weigh her? Why is he spitting up? Is she colicky?

Let go and don't worry.

Does he feel warm? Does she look sick? Feel his first tooth. Don't leave him alone. That might choke him. Is the pacifier clean? Should we call the doctor? We can't make it, because the baby isn't feeling well. Stay with her in case she gets worse.

Let go and don't worry.

She likes it when you sing. He goes to bed at eight. Rock her for a little while. Rub his back to calm him down. Please warm his bottle. Here are our phone numbers. We won't be out late. Make sure you lock the door. Give him one last kiss. Don't forget to tickle her feet. Keep him in your mind in case he needs you.

Let go and call to check on her later.

Make sure you put a hat on him. She needs her favorite blanket. Turn the table so he won't hit his head. Don't let her touch that. Watch she doesn't wobble too much.

Maybe we should put a pillow behind him. Hold your hands behind her so you can catch her when she falls.

Let go and watch her sit up all by herself

Pick up the rug so she won't trip. Lock the cabinets. Buy a baby gate. Make sure she eats lunch. She didn't eat much breakfast. He's fast so don't turn your back for a moment. Is the car seat in tight enough? Prop up his head so he won't hurt his neck. Tie his shoe so he doesn't trip. Stand behind him and catch him in case he falls.

Let go of his hand so he can stand up.

Move the rocks out of the way. Feel the grass and see if it is wet. Pick up the rug, so he doesn't trip. She isn't too steady yet. Should she be pulling herself up? Move the unsteady stuff. Buy soft shoes. Smooth the corners. Pave the way. Watch the steps.

That looks slippery. Follow behind so you can catch him if he falls.

Let go and let her walk.

Hurry behind him. Is he okay? Pick him up. Brush off the dirt. Kiss where it hurts. A Band-aid will make it better. Don't hover. Tell him it will be okay. Put him back down. Let her try it again. Grit your teeth. Say a prayer. Stay closer this time to catch her if she falls.

Let go and let him try again.

Buy a lunchbox. Hem his uniform pants. Print her name on her supplies. Talk about school. Pack the backpack. Make a good breakfast. Calm the butterflies. Put a ribbon in her hair. Show him how to open his snack. Meet the teacher. Walk him to the door.

Kiss her head. Wave goodbye. Watch from the bushes in case he falls.

Let go so she can start school.

Buy a helmet. Show him how to pedal. Hold on. Run after her. Keep looking ahead. Pedal faster. Keep going. Pedal faster. I'm right behind you. I won't let go. You're doing great. Make it steady. Run close to him so you can catch him in case he falls.

Let go and watch him ride all by himself.

Let go and let him fail so he will learn.

Stay close so you can help him begin again.

Let go and trust she will be okay driving by herself.

Stay close in case she calls and needs you.

Let go and leave him at school.

Call and make sure he is okay when he is in your thoughts.

Let go and don't worry if she is late.

Stay close to the phone and ignore the pounding of your heart.

Let go now, he doesn't need you.

Stay close, he always needs a mother.

A Prayer for Mothers

I pray for mothers everywhere.

For good mothers and mothers whose best will never be quite good enough.

For mothers who easily fall in love with their babies before they are born, and mothers who fumble and struggle to figure out how they will measure up.

For mothers whose joy overflows as they hold healthy robust newborns, and for those who must search for a memory because they must say goodbye so quickly.

I pray for mothers who patiently rock crying babies all night, and for those tired and impatient mothers who cry right along with their baby.

For first-time mothers and mothers whose hands and hearts are already full.

For the mothers who wonder how they will feed their hungry children, and mothers who must helplessly sit and watch their children starve themselves.

I pray for those whose children breeze through school, and for mothers who watch their children work hard, only to struggle and fail.

I pray for mothers who rethink milestones and rejoice at smaller steps than others do.

For mothers who can trust their children, and for mothers who constantly worry.

I pray for mothers who are able to stay at home with their children, and those who must trust their care to someone else.

I pray for mothers who must raise their children alone, and mothers who are courageous enough to swallow their pride and ask for help.

I pray for mothers who know they won't live to see their child grow up, and mothers who lovingly adopt another mother's children, just because.

I pray for mothers who cry for safety as they raise children in time of war, and mothers who battle against drugs and violence.

And for those whose children scream, "I hate you," when they are mad, and for those mothers who would kill to hear their child say even one word.

I pray for mothers who must fight prejudice and language barriers and hate, and for those who wonder how they will ever teach their children to appreciate freedom.

And I pray for mothers who must face judgment and stares, because they have chosen life, and for those mothers who bear the burden of their choice silently.